Read for a
Better World

RAMADAN AND EID AL-FITR
A First Look

PERCY LEED

GRL Consultant, Diane Craig, Certified Literacy Specialist
Content Consultant, Mun'im Sirry, Professor of Theology, University of Notre Dame

Lerner Publications ◆ Minneapolis

Educator Toolbox

Reading books is a great way for kids to express what they're interested in. Before reading this title, ask the reader these questions:

What do you think this book is about? Look at the cover for clues.

What do you already know about Ramadan and Eid al-Fitr?

What do you want to learn about Ramadan and Eid al-Fitr?

Let's Read Together

Encourage the reader to use the pictures to understand the text.

Point out when the reader successfully sounds out a word.

Praise the reader for recognizing sight words such as *is* and *they*.

TABLE OF CONTENTS

Ramadan and Eid al-Fitr . . . 4

Ramadan and Eid al-Fitr

Ramadan lasts for one month.

Muslims have
a holy book.
They read it
at this time.

People pray five
times a day.

People fast.
They do not
eat or drink.
They fast from
dawn to sunset.

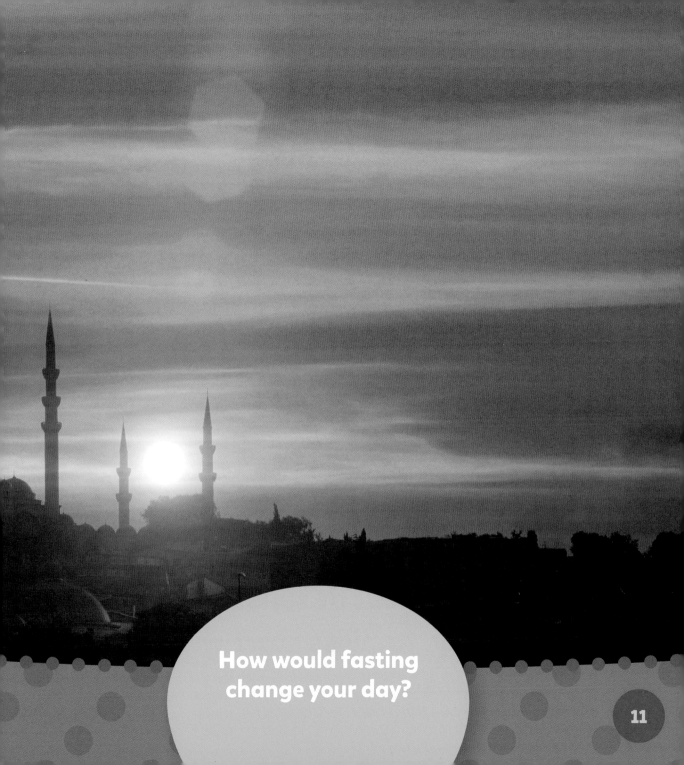

How would fasting
change your day?

People eat at sunset.
Some families start with
dates and water.

They pray.
Then they eat
a full meal.

The month ends.
Eid al-Fitr starts.
People dress up.

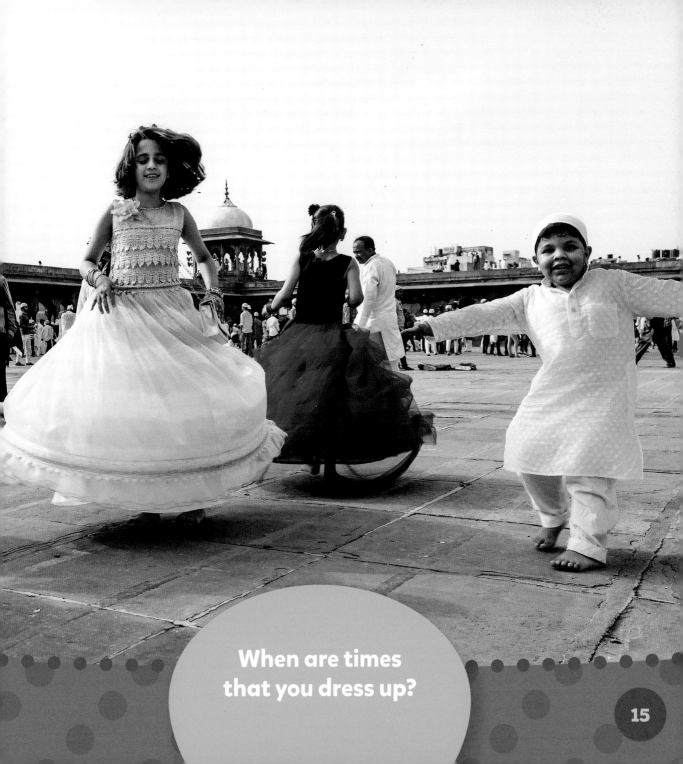

When are times
that you dress up?

They pray together.

People give gifts.
They give to
the poor.

Why do you think people give to the poor at this time?

19

Ramadan is for faith.
Eid al-Fitr is for giving thanks.

You Connect!

Do you celebrate Ramadan and Eid al-Fitr?

When are times of year that you give thanks?

What is something you have done or would like to do for Ramadan or Eid al-Fitr?

Social and Emotional Snapshot

Student voice is crucial to building reader confidence. Ask the reader:

What is your favorite part of this book?

What is something you learned from this book?

Did this book remind you of any other holidays you celebrate?

Opportunities for social and emotional learning are everywhere. How can you connect the topic of this book to the SEL competencies below?

Self-Awareness
Relationship Skills
Social Awareness

Photo Glossary

dates

holy book

pray

sunset

Learn More

Leed, Percy. *Diwali: A First Look*. Minneapolis: Lerner Publications, 2023.

Lumbard, Rabiah York. *The Gift of Ramadan*. Chicago: Albert Whitman & Company, 2019.

Schuh, Mari. *Crayola Ramadan and Eid al-Fitr Colors*. Minneapolis: Lerner Publications, 2019.

Index

Photo Acknowledgments

The images in this book are used with the permission of: © PeopleImages/iStockphoto, pp. 4–5; © ferlistockphoto/iStockphoto, pp. 6–7, 23 (top right); © Alex Liew/iStockphoto, p. 8; © nazar_ab/iStockphoto, pp. 8–9, 23 (bottom left); © Maxiphoto/iStockphoto, pp. 10–11, 23 (bottom right); © HAKAN ELİAÇIK/iStockphoto, pp. 12, 23 (top left); © Boontoom Sae-Kor/Shutterstock Images, p. 13; © Sauvik Acharyya/Shutterstock Images, pp. 14–15; © sabirmallick/iStockphoto, pp. 16–17; © Gulcin Ragiboglu/iStockphoto, p. 18; © JOAT/Shutterstock Images, pp. 18–19; © arapix/Shutterstock Images, p. 20.

Cover Photo: © arapix/iStockphoto.

Design Elements: © Mighty Media, Inc.

Lerner Publications Company
An imprint of Lerner Publishing Group, Inc.
241 First Avenue North
Minneapolis, MN 55401 USA

For reading levels and more information, look up this title at www.lernerbooks.com.

Main body text set in Mikado a Medium.
Typeface provided by Hannes von Doehren.

Library of Congress Cataloging-in-Publication Data

Names: Leed, Percy, 1968– author.
Title: Ramadan and Eid al-Fitr : a first look / Percy Leed.
Description: Minneapolis : Lerner Publications , 2023. | Series: Read about holidays (read for a better world) | Includes bibliographical references and index. | Audience: Ages 5–8 | Audience: Grades K–1 | Summary: "Ramadan and Eid al-Fitr celebrate faith and giving thanks. Through thoughtful text and critical-thinking questions, readers will learn all about these two holidays and how people celebrate them"– Provided by publisher.
Identifiers: LCCN 2022009022 (print) | LCCN 2022009023 (ebook) | ISBN 9781728475653 (library binding) | ISBN 9781728478982 (paperback) | ISBN 9781728484266 (ebook)
Subjects: LCSH: Ramadan–Juvenile literature. | Eid al-Fitr–Juvenile literature. | Fasts and feasts–Islam–Juvenile literature.
Classification: LCC BP186.4 .L44 2023 (print) | LCC BP186.4 (ebook) | DDC 394.265/7–dc23/eng20220527

LC record available at https://lccn.loc.gov/2022009022
LC ebook record available at https://lccn.loc.gov/2022009023

Manufactured in the United States of America
1 – CG – 12/15/22